# AIN'T LIFE AN ARTICHOKE?

## IT TAKES A LOT OF PEELING TO GET TO THE HEART ... THE STUFF RELATIONSHIPS ARE MADE OF

### BY DR. LINDA ANDRADE WHEELER

### ILLUSTRATED BY JOE HUNT
### EDITED BY M. GARRETT WHEELER

Much gratitude is extended to Milton Wheeler and Noelani Schilling for their suggestions and scrutiny of this book; Lance Wheeler, who answered a lot of "What do you think?" questions in the course of writing this book; and of course, Garrett Wheeler, whose attention to the technical aspects of publishing made this book possible.

Edited by M. Garrett Wheeler
Illustrated by Joe Hunt

Published by
The Human Connection, Inc.
1210 Auahi Street, Suite 231,
Honolulu, Hawaii 96814.
Telephone number (808) 593-8812.
For further information or additional copies, contact
The Human Connection Inc.

Library of Congress Catalog Card Number: 96-090851
ISBN: 09639713-3-6

*To my husband Milt,*

*Who continually reminds me of the lei made of young avocados that won me an award for creativity in elementary school. It was a symbol of my courage to be different — to be unique.*


*To my sons,*

*Whom I love deeply. This book could not be written without the love, inspiration, encouragement and support you have given me throughout my life. You have made my personal journey to the heart — a once-in-a lifetime experience — worth repeating.*

# Contents

**A** cquire a sharper vision of your life. Decide what you really want and commit yourself to getting it. Focus fresh attention to it daily.

**R** isk to reach your loftiest goal. Think big. Try something new everyday and share that with others. You are a unique individual with unlimited potential.

**T** each others and learn from them. Share what you know and be open to the perspectives of others. Accept yourself where you are, but work regularly at growing each and every day.

**I** nvolve yourself in life. Look at the world with wide-eyed wonder. Greet each day with anticipation and expectation.

**C** ommunicate to build relationships. Cultivate friendships that are meaningful to you and motivates others. The relationship you build or destroy is always your own.

**H** elp others to grow. Give people the opportunity to excel. Make them feel important and special in your company.

**O** perate with optimism. Develop a positive attitude, a healthy sense of humor, and a pattern of effective habits.

**K** now what to look for and understand what you see. Maximize the moments of truth to create happy memories.

**E** xcel within yourself by always being your best self. Your uniqueness is your greatest asset.

 **The Human Connection**
© 1996 Dr. Linda Andrade Wheeler      800-471-9808

# Preface

This book is about self-discovery and self-renewal in the process of building healthy & happy relationships. It is about a journey to one's heart, which each person must take alone to find their own uniqueness. The process can be uplifting and bring a brand new perspective to life. A person's uniqueness is at the heart of their existence. To discover that is to make the most valuable contribution to oneself and others. It is the special gift a person brings into this world. To discover the things that touch our hearts and share that with others is to experience the best part of living. It is a gift you give yourself and others throughout your life.

The artichoke is used as a metaphor to demonstrate the layers of reality associated with relationships, that we need to peel away to get to our uniqueness — with all its richness— so we can feel special and share that specialness with others. It is the heart of the artichoke that we patiently work towards when we choose that delicacy to enjoy. Similarly, it is when we love and serve others, and build relationships that nurture our growth as better human beings, that we know we have discovered the best of us — our hearts .

Once we enjoy the feeling and benefits that heart-felt relationships add to our lives, we can no longer look at others, and not want to discover the very best of them – their hearts. The peeling process is the test of our patience and commitment to ourselves and the value we place on other human beings.

Enjoy the journey as you peel away — layer by layer — to get to the best of you.

## 24 Golden Hours

*Every morning you are handed 24 golden hours.*

*They are one of the few things in this world that you get free of charge.*

*If you had all the money in the world, you couldn't buy one extra hour.*

*What will you do with this priceless treasure?*

*Remember, you must use it, because it is given only once.*

*Once wasted, you can never get it back.*

*– Anonymous*

# Introduction

*AIN'T LIFE AN ARTICHOKE?*
*It Takes a Lot of Peeling to*
*Get to the Heart ... The Stuff that*
*Relationships are Made of...*

No matter where we are in life, we interact with people. — How well we interact with others will ultimately determine the quality of our relationships. We've all heard the expression, "when people like you they will help you to succeed, if they don't like you, they don't care if you fail." People generally need to know that what they are doing makes a difference in their life. Having the support of others makes the process of living more enjoyable, worthwhile and satisfying.

Success in life involves having a sense of who we are, how well we do in what we do, and the quality of our relationships. We are likely to see ourselves in terms of our roles, responsibilities and relationships. Ultimately, what counts most in life is how we feel about ourselves and what we do for people.

As wonderful as we may be, we need to surround ourselves with good, supportive people. Then and only then, can we make significant things happen. We must embrace the diversity of people and welcome their differences. Today, the problem is not how to become alike, but it is how we can co-exist together for positive results in our many arenas in life.

Our attitude about ourselves and our relationships are a matter of choice. Think how hard it is to change ourselves, then we can better understand what little chance we have of changing others. Before we go about peeling away the layers of others, we need to peel away the many layers of our own realities that we have accumulated throughout our lives. By peeling away layers of our own notion of reality, with all of its biases, prejudices and stereotypes, we get a clearer picture of who we are, how we feel about things and a sense of where we would like to be. This takes courage, strength and the willingness to open ourselves to self-examination, self-discovery and self-renewal.

A major reason capable people fail to advance in what they are doing is because they do not work well other people. Our ability to handle people — how we communicate with them, how effectively we interact with them and to what degree we empathize with them — will determine the quality of our relationships on a personal and professional level.

Our success in attaining the quality of life that keeps us growing, happy, and challenged depends entirely upon ourselves. Our success in life depends on how much we put into it and the focus we give it. The thing with success is that we need to work hard to get it, it's not likely to fall in our laps just thinking about it. Our dreams and how far we can dream is as far as we will go. That's the power of imagination! It's a self-fulling prophecy that how we see ourselves and what we think we deserve will eventually be our reality — the world we create for ourselves.

Like the artichoke, we have just one life to live. Our life is not a practice run — a warm up for the real thing. Remember, the years will go by anyway. We can choose to drift along — that's easy — or we can work hard to get what we want out of life. How we go about living and shaping our lives determines the quality of our life-style and ultimately, our degree of happiness.

This book will present a "peeling" thought for each of the letters contained in the word ARTICHOKE, followed by some quotes to "peel" by. It is hoped that when our readers look at another artichoke they will see more than its prickly, yet tasty leaves. That when "peeled" layer by layer, they can enjoy the process of discovery, and eventually to rejoice in the pleasure of tasting it to its fullest

— its heart.

**A**quire a sharper vision of your life. Decide what you really want and commit yourself to getting it. Focus fresh attention to it daily.

"Is this really what I want?" That is one of the first questions we need to ask ourselves before making a choice. Most often, the reason individuals can't get the thing that they think they want — both in their personal and professional lives — is because they're not sure if they really want it. When making a choice, we need to weigh what we may gain, against what we will have to give up. We need to be careful with what we choose to pursue, because we may get it. After all, we are who we are by the choices we make. Destiny is not a matter of chance, but a matter of choice.

People who succeed in their chosen paths, somehow have learned an important lesson about achievement. They consciously or unconsciously follow certain steps to achieve whatever they desire. Successful people know that quality has no finish line, and that once they achieve something, they continue on their path to achieving another goal. Meanwhile, they take care of what they already have that brought them success.

There are definite steps determined people are likely to take on their way to success. First, they are very precise in what it is they are after in life. They know what they really want and this clear vision gives them the power to put it in sharper focus; secondly, because they know that desire or wishing for something is not enough, they take action towards their goal; thirdly, they are energy-focused. They do not want to continue to expend their personal power on any approach they feel is worthless in attaining their goal. They know when

something is working or not ; and
fourthly, they are flexible and open-
minded.  They will not stick to an
approach that does not bring positive
results.  Successful people change their
approach continually until they achieve
what they want.

Quotes to "peel" by....

There are two things to
aim for in life: first, to get
what you want; and after
that to enjoy it. Only
the wisest of people
achieve the second.

❧ ❧ ❧

Vision is the art of seeing
things invisible.

❧ ❧ ❧

A vision is the answer
to the question,"What do
I want?" Your vision is
not a goal. Setting a
goal is how you work
toward your vision.

Work hard to get
what you want
and when you get
it, take care of it.

❧ ❧ ❧

A goal without
action is a dream;
all action without
a goal is passing time;
and a goal
with action is
accomplishment.

❧ ❧ ❧

Focus on what
you want, and what
you focus on you
will get.

There are times when the greatest change needed is a change of your viewpoint.

ぞ ぞ ぞ

The people who get on in this world are the people who get up and look for the circumstances they want, and if they can't find them, make them.

ぞ ぞ ぞ

Where you are is where you choose to be. If you don't like where you are at today, make better choices so you can be happy.

The visionary
is the only true realist.

❧ ❧ ❧

You are limited less by
luck, by heredity or by
circumstances, than
by your own capacity
to envision the
very best you can be.

❧ ❧ ❧

Some people want
success to happen;
some wish success
would happen;
while others make
things happen for
their success.

We are who we are
by the choices
we make.
Everything
you need
for a happy
life is within you.

🐌 🐌 🐌

Hang on to your dreams,
they become your reality.

🐌 🐌 🐌

If you don't know where
you are going, you'll never
know if you've arrived.

🐌 🐌 🐌

## *Let Me*

Let me be a little kinder.
Let me be a little blinder
To the faults of those about me;
Let me be, when I am weary,
Just a litttle bit more cheery;
Let me serve a little better those
That I am striving for.

Let me be a little braver
When temptation bids me waver;
Let me strive a little harder
To be all that I should be;
Let me be a little meeker
With the person that is weaker;
Let me think more of my neighbor
And a little less of me.

*– Anonymous*

**R**isk to reach your loftiest goal. Think Big. Try something new everyday and share that with others. You are a unique individual with unlimited potential.

Personal growth is a process of trial and error. Each day we have the opportunity to learn lessons. There are no mistakes in life, just lessons designed to make us better, not bitter. We may like the lessons and learn from them, or think them stupid or irrevelant. Too many of us drop out of the game of life because of the idea that a "winner" is someone who never loses, when in fact, all of our "failed" experiments are as much a part of the process as the experiments that ultimately "works" for us.

The only permanent thing we face in life is constant change. Change offers both uncertainity and opportunity. How we manage ourselves will make all the difference in viewing change as an opportunity that can create a climate of personal growth and satisfying results.

We can face change and manage it by developing new perspectives, looking for opportunities in difficult times, and challenging our potential and creativity to meet the changes. By doing this, we can feel good about moving on to new and better experiences and relationships. Those who know how to react in a climate of constant change, will not only survive life's adjustments, but they position themselves to succeed. The key to handling change is to gain control of ourselves and difficult situations that invariably will arise.

People who pursue their dreams believe in themselves. They know their actions make a difference in their lives and the lives of others. They work hard at trusting themselves and others. They do not allow their dreams to evaporate into nothingness.  Of what value are ideas if they are allowed to die? Perhaps, people who do not bring their dreams to fruition, feel they are not worthy of them.  The sad thing about this is, these people think so little of their ideas that when a new idea is once again conceived, it can never be born and nurtured to greatness because of their lack of belief in themselves.

Quotes to "peel" by...

Everybody's
somebody special.
Treat everyone
that way all the
time, everywhere.

🐦 🐦 🐦

You have
everything
you need —
knowledge,
skills, attitude
& feelings —
to be successful
and happy in life.
What you do with
your gifts is up to
you.  The choice
is yours.

Have you noticed that
in life what
sometimes appears to
be the end of something
is really a new beginning?

❧ ❧ ❧

You are not limited by
one chance, everyday you
are blessed with a
new beginning.

❧ ❧ ❧

Your attitude is a
matter of choice.
You make the difference
in your life.

Failure is the
opportunity to begin
again, more intelligently.

❧ ❧ ❧

The highest
compliment anyone
can give another human
being is to expect the
very best of them —
because you have
such faith in them.

❧ ❧ ❧

Successful people do
not have the word
"failure"
in their dictionary.

Anyone can handle nice
people; it is the difficult
people who make
relationships a challenge.

≈ ≈ ≈

Difficult people are like
diamonds in the rough —
they need to be polished
and gently worked with to
be at their best.

≈ ≈ ≈

Share laughter,
time and knowledge
with others.  It brings
people closer
together as
human beings.

Give people a chance to
see the meaningful
results of their efforts.
They will grow in
enthusiasm and will
desire to do things
they can be proud of
accomplishing.

ᴈ ᴈ ᴈ

Education is the ability
to listen to almost
anything without
losing your temper
or self-confidence.

ᴈ ᴈ ᴈ

Don't just survive.
Flourish. Thrive.

A failure a day
keeps
complacency
and
arrogance
away.

જ જ જ

We all have one life;
but there are many
ways of living it.

જ જ જ

Only those
who risk
going too far
can possibly
find out how far
they can go.

We are limited
not by who
we think we are;
but who we think
we are not.

əa. əa. əa.

We think
of success and
failure as opposites,
yet they are not.
Without experiencing
failure, how could we
experience the
exuberance of success.
They are necessary
experiences to help
us appreciate our
investment in ourselves
and in life.

There is no single "right"
way of being human.
There are many options
that are open to you.
It is your choice
as to what kind of
human being you
want to be.

❧ ❧ ❧

Losers make excuses.
Winners make progress.

❧ ❧ ❧

Create
an environment
where failure is not fatal.
It is an ability to fail that
makes for lasting success.

&&& &&& &&&

What you are
is God's gift to you.
What you make of it
is your gift to God.

&&& &&& &&&

### *Risk*

To laugh is to risk appearing the fool.
To weep is to risk appearing sentimental.
To reach out for another is to risk
  involvement.
To expose feelings is to risk exposing
  your true self.
To place your ideas, your dreams before the
  crowd, is to risk their loss.
To love is to risk not being loved
  in return.
To live is to risk dying.
To hope is to risk despair.
To try is to risk failure.

But risks must be taken because the greatest
hazzard in life is to risk nothing.  People
who risk nothing, have nothing, are nothing.
People who risk nothing cannot learn, feel,
change, grow, love... live.  Chained by
their certitudes, they are slaves, they have
forfeited freedom.
Only a person who risks is free.

*– Anonymous*

### *Everybody's Somebody Special*

Whenever you think of yourself,
Remember the special person that you are.
No one is exactly like you in the whole
   world.
Your uniqueness is a gift you share
   with others.
It is your influencing statement in life —
the personal impression you leave
   with others.
Know that everyone you meet will have
   their own gifts to share.
Let them be proud of their offerings.
Give each person the opportunity to be
   their best self,
And you will enjoy the specialness
   of everyone.

*– LAW*

Teach others and learn from them. Share what you know and be open to the perspectives of others. Accept yourself and where you are, but work regularly at growing each and everyday.

Human interaction is a learning experience. More importantly, human interaction must be viewed as a growing process, in which something that may be helpful, refreshing, informational or illuminating is exchanged between two or more people for the sole purpose of making them better human beings.

Successful people are committed to ongoing learning and growth. They give back by teaching and helping others. They know that when they teach others they learn even more intensely about the subject they are teaching. People who help others become better learners, experience growth themselves.

People who give and get the most out of life are those, who, in addition to their other qualities, have two things in

common.  First, they do whatever they
are doing with passion and secondly,
they experience a special satisfaction in
being helpful to other people.

Quotes to "peel" by...

Teach others to value each
other as human beings.

❧ ❧ ❧

It is when you give of
yourself that you
truly give to others.

❧ ❧ ❧

Help people become
more motivated by
guiding them to the source
of their own power.

❧ ❧ ❧

Empower yourself and
you will empower
those around you.

To know and not to act, is
not to know at all.

❧ ❧ ❧

People feel motivated
and proud when they
believe they are doing
meaningful work.

❧ ❧ ❧

If two people
always agree, what is
the use of one?

❧ ❧ ❧

Help others make
sound decisions.

The kindness, concern and good humor you share with others will have a strong impact on them.

❧ ❧ ❧

People skills are developed through the heart, not the head.

❧ ❧ ❧

Bad things sometimes happen to good people — broken dreams, broken visions and broken hearts. We need to have a reserve of good feelings about ourselves to fuel our lives towards success.

Honest differences are
often a healthy sign
of progress.

❧ ❧ ❧

I am working ...
you just can't see it.

❧ ❧ ❧

We need to learn to share
our personal power with
others and to build bridges
rather than close doors.

❧ ❧ ❧

It is impossible
to teach
on an empty spirit.

A sign
of a truly
educated person
is the ability to
hear many diverse
viewpoints and not
get ruffled by any.

🐌 🐌 🐌

Who you are
and how you act conveys
more about you
than anything
you will ever say.

🐌 🐌 🐌

To share and enjoy each
other's "ahas" is one of
life's precious gifts.

To be praised is a
basic human desire.
Be generous with
your praise and pass it
around freely.
The supply is limited
only by you.

૨૦ ૨૦ ૨૦

I don't care
what you learn —
present yourself
as a learner.

૨૦ ૨૦ ૨૦

Doing your best is
more important than
being the best.

Work hard
to be super competent
in your area of expertise
so that your advice
and counsel
can be trusted.

❧ ❧ ❧

It is a funny thing
about life;
if you refuse
to accept anything
but the best, you
often get it.

❧ ❧ ❧

Help others
whenever you can.

No one is powerless.
Sociologists point out
that even the most
introverted adult
influences over
10,000 people in
his/her lifetime.

❧ ❧ ❧

Little things don't
mean a lot, they
mean everything.

❧ ❧ ❧

Transplanted people,
like plants,
need extra care
in the beginning
to fully take root.

## Who Makes the Group a Success?

Xvxn though my typxwritxr is an old modxl, it works quitx wxll, xxcxpt for onx or two kxys. I havx wishxd many timxs that it workxd pxrfxctly. It is trux that thxrx arx forty-six kxys that function wxll xnough, but just onx kxy not working makxs thx diffxrxncx.

Somxtimxs our group is somxwhat likx my typxwritxr, not all thx kxy pxoplx arx working propxrly. You may say to yoursxlf, "wxll, I am only onx pxrson, I won't makx or brxak thx group." But it doxs makx a diffxrxncx, bxcausx a group, to bx xffxctivx, nxxds thx activx participation of xvxry pxrson. So thx nxxt timx you think that you arx only onx pxrson and that your xfforts arx not nxxdxd, rxmxmbxr my typxwritxr and say to yoursxlf, "I'm a kxy pxrson in thx group, and I am nxxdxd vxry much."

*(This illustrates that who you are makes a difference — and like the typewriter, with just one key[e] missing, any group with only one member not functioning properly will make a big difference in the effectiveness of that group.)*

43

*Involve yourself in life. Look at the world with wide-eyed wonder; greet each day with anticipation and expectation.*

The most important quality of life is the value of life itself. Therefore, we must learn to love our life — not just spend it. It's just a matter of fact that all people eventually die, but only few of them really live their lives to the fullest — with innovative ideas, exciting people and things that nurture their personal growth. People who really live see everyday as a new chance at life.

We need to take time to remember what it is to live in the present, totally absorbed in what is going on in life -to pause from time to time and ponder on the good things in life by letting your senses respond to a song, a smile, the splatter of raindrops, the touch of a hand, or the whisper of leaves rippled by a warm summer breeze. If we watch children interacting with nature and with others, what we see is an unedited version of reality. Children still have the marvelous spirit of adventure and believe life is good and they are capable beings. As adults, we tend to build layers of artificial limitations that keep us from being at our best everytime.

Somehow many of us pay more attention to the artificial culture that limits our personal growth, When in fact, we ought to give more serious attention to the culture that comes from within us. The culture inside of us is our own creation – it is the one we feel with our hearts, not see with our eyes. It is a powerful force as to how we view our world, the people in it, and ourselves. It is the only real culture that

counts as far as being a caring and
compassionate human being.

Our creativity is limited only by
our own ingenuity and imagination. We
must be willing to leave our comfort
zones -- to explore the new and unfa-
miliar. Creative people always have an
unexhaustible supply of imaginative
energy, and surround themselves with
fresh ideas and interesting people to
stimulate and encourage this kind of
perspective in life.

They are consciously tuned into
the precious moments, when important
things are happening — a flower
blooming, an animal being born, a child
at play, the breaking of a wave,  a
bridegroom's expression at seeing his
new bride walk down the aisle, etc. To

observe these kinds of things on a
regular basis  is to be an active partici-
pant in life, not just a spectator.

Quotes to "peel" by...

They call today the
present, because it is
truly a gift that you
are here to experience
the joy of today.

🐌 🐌 🐌

We need to find and
invent ways to keep
in touch with the
sky, sun and sea,
and understand the
sacredness
of these things.

🐌 🐌 🐌

Life is not a problem
to be solved; but a
solution to be experienced.

Respond with all of
your senses to the
miracles of the natural
world.  People can be
physically and mentally
present in the place
they choose to be.

🐸 🐸 🐸

If you worry about what
might be, and wonder
what might have been,
you will ignore what is.

🐸 🐸 🐸

The optimist proclaims
that we live in the best of
all worlds. The pessimist
fears this is true.

The world is full of
remarkable and exciting
things to see and do,
to taste, feel and touch.
Do not miss the splendor
of seeing them
with clear and new eyes.

🐦 🐦 🐦

Trust yourself.  Act
on what you think is right.

🐦 🐦 🐦

One's perception of reality
can be whatever one
chooses. Image is the style
of thoughts —the way
you choose to dress,
think and act.

Life is
10%
what happens
to me and
90%
how I react to it.

🐸 🐸 🐸

Be the best
wherever you are
and with whoever
you are with
at the time.

🐸 🐸 🐸

Take life seriously.
Experience it
every day and
in every way.

Positive action brings
positive results.
Remember, if you plant
pineapples, you can expect
pineapples at harvest time,
not papayas.

ᐒ ᐒ ᐒ

Respect yourself.
Appreciate and be
proud of your talents,
expertise and differences.

ᐒ ᐒ ᐒ

Especially with
loved ones, remember
that nothing lasts forever.
Live each day as if it were
your last day with them.

### *It's Up To You*

Have you made someone happy,
Or made someone sad?
What have you done
With the day that you had?

God gave it to you
To do just as you would,
Did you do what was wicked,
Or do what was good?

Did you hand out a smile
Or give them a frown?
Did you lift someone up
Or push someone down?

Did you lighten some load
Or some progress impede?
Did you look for a rose
Or just gather a weed?

What did you do
With the beautiful day?
God gave it to you
Did you throw it away?

*– Anonymous*

### *Today is The Very First Day of the Rest of My Life*

This is the beginning of a new day.
God has given me this day to use as I will.

I can waste it...or use it for good, but
what I do today is important, because
I am exchanging a day of my life for it!

When tomorrow comes, this day will be
gone forever, leaving in its place something
that I have traded for it.

I want it to be gain, not loss; good
and not evil; success, and not failure;
in order that I shall not regret the
price that I have paid for it. I will try
just for today, for you never fail
until you stop trying.

*– Anonymous*

*Communicate to build relationships. Cultivate friendships that are meaningful to you and motivates others. The relationship you build or destroy is always your own.*

Communication is at the heart of interpersonal relationships – it is shared meaning between two or more people. And language is at the heart of communication. However, communication is more than a language process, it is a people process that is used to establish and nurture lasting relationships.

How well we communicate determines the quality of our relationships. The more successful we are at communicating with someone, the closer our relationship will be to that person. However, one of the biggest barriers to effective communications is the assumption that the other person understands us. If we are in doubt, then we ought to ask the appropriate questions so that our messages are interpreted correctly.

It is our responsibility to make sure we are communicating effectively. Whenever and with whomever we communicate, it becomes our responsibility to be sure we have been clearly understood. Not only do we send messages, but we also receive them, so we are aware of clues that tell us if our messages were received correctly or if they were misinterpreted.

A recent study showed that the average married couple has only 20 minutes of meaningful conversation with their spouses or companions per week. The major culprit was time. Therefore, it becomes essential for people to continue to communicate effectively in order to nurture relationships in spite of very real obstacles that put limitations on their communications. People with busy careers, children, elderly parents, financial responsibilities, and community obligations must take time to communicate on a regular basis to keep their relationships healthy and happy.

The power of communicating successfully with others is, sometimes, we can actually change people's attitudes and behaviors. Also, it must be remembered that because communication is a people process, we need to know, understand and practice sound human relations.

Quotes to "peel" by...

Communication is
at the core of all human
relationships —
just as the heart is to
a human being, as
rice is to the riceball;
as dough is to bread,
as wings are to the
airplane; and as the
engine is to a car.

❧ ❧ ❧

Understand that happiness
is not based on
possessions,
power or
prestige,
but on
relationships with people
you love and respect.

Make friends
even when you
don't need them.

❧ ❧ ❧

If two people always
agree, what is the
use of one?

❧ ❧ ❧

In order to have a
friend, be one.

❧ ❧ ❧

The word "Please"
is a great
lubricator
for human relations.

The best way to destroy
an enemy is to make
him/her your friend.

࿇ ࿇ ࿇

Criticism is a quick way
to destroy a friendship or
even make enemies.

࿇ ࿇ ࿇

The wise aren't
always silent, but they
know when to be.

࿇ ࿇ ࿇

Pay less attention to
what people say; but
watch what they do.

Hearing is a gift that God gives us; listening is a skill that we develop and perfect.

❧ ❧ ❧

Be an active listener to show others that you care, and you might learn something in the process too!

❧ ❧ ❧

"We" language is more effective than "I" language in a group.

❧ ❧ ❧

The words you use shape your image.

Smiling is a universal
language.  We all smile in
the same language.

🐌 🐌 🐌

To get people to understand
you, send them clear,
concise, correct, complete
and comprehensive
messages.
Avoid mixed signals
that lead to
miscommunication
and misinterpretation.

🐌 🐌 🐌

Keep people informed.
When information stops,
rumors start.

Words have wings to
carry us to our
highest dreams.
Use positive and action
words to "pump"
yourself up with
energy to make your
dreams come true.

❧ ❧ ❧

Words are the voice
of the heart; eyes are the
windows to the soul.

❧ ❧ ❧

A male falls in love
through his eyes.
A female falls in love
through her ears.

Who you are
and how you act
conveys more about
you than anything
you will ever say.

🙂 🙂 🙂

Women say that
men never listen.
Men say that women
listen too intently
to every detail —
they never forget.

🙂 🙂 🙂

God gave us two ears
and one mouth.
Perhaps He was trying to
tell us something.

Speak and act
as if everything
you did was
a genuine concern.
Be approachable,
friendly, concerned
and respectful.

🐌 🐌 🐌

Be sure your actions
speak for you.
Who you are
speaks louder
than your words.

🐌 🐌 🐌

Some people will
believe anything —
if you whisper it.

Avoid arguments
with others.
In difficult
situations, we all
have two choices:
1) retaliate or
2) stay calm
and listen.
Anger is low level
brain function.
Most people don't make
a lot of sense when
they're angry.
So, if you stay calm and
listen, you may
understand the person's
point of view, smooth
some feathers, and have
an opportunity to
share your
viewpoint as well.

Don't talk unless you can
improve the silence.

❧ ❧ ❧

So often we say I love you
with a big I and a small
you.

❧ ❧ ❧

*Help others to grow. Give people the opportunity to excel. Make them feel important and special in your company.*

Wherever there is a human being, there is an opportunity for kindness. When you help to make people feel important, they act important, and they produce positive results! Someone once said that you will get everything in life that you want, if you will help enough people to get what they want. That makes sense to me, because whatever you give out always seems to come back to you, even at times when you least expect them. So if we consciously help other people to succeed — not necessarily with the notion of getting anything back — their usual response is to want to help you in return.

There are no perfect people in the world, so we must accept people exactly as they are. Concentrate on people's good points and help them to strengthen areas they want to improve. Be someone who supports the efforts of others by positioning yourself as an ally, not an adversary.

Praise people for what they have done. It is amazing what people can do when they are valued, appreciated and acknowledged for their contributions. On the other hand, criticism is a quick way to destroy a friendship or even make enemies.

Quotes to "peel" by...

A person cannot
antagonize and
influence at the
same time.

≥≥ ≥≥ ≥≥

People like you
to the extent
that they
feel comfortable in
your presence.

≥≥ ≥≥ ≥≥

Friendship
should not be
thought of as
something we get.
It is something
we give.

Forgiveness
may not
change the past,
but it can
enlarge
your future.

🐸 🐸 🐸

Create
an environment
where failure
is not fatal.
It is an ability
to fail
that makes for
lasting
relationships
between and
among people.

Two things are bad
for the heart:
Running uphill and
running down people.

ả ả ả

There are people
who, by their
very presence,
make others feel
important, alive
and capable
of becoming
someone better
than they had
ever been before.
Wouldn't you like
to make people
feel that way?

You make more friends
by becoming interested
in other people than
by trying to interest
other people in you.

🐌 🐌 🐌

The love in your heart
wasn't put there to stay.
Love isn't love till
it's given away.

🐌 🐌 🐌

Help others
to make their
dreams come true.
Keep telling people
positive things for
them to succeed.

Have you ever noticed
that when someone acts
important, they are treated
with a great deal more
respect than people
who lack confidence
in themselves?

ॐ ॐ ॐ

Wherever you are,
provide an environment
which empowers others
to succeed.

ॐ ॐ ॐ

It is not fair to ask
of others what you
are not willing to
do yourself.

Help others
whenever you can.

🐦 🐦 🐦

People need love
the most when they
deserve it the least.

🐦 🐦 🐦

The highest
compliment anyone
can give another
human being
is to expect the
best of them,
because you have
such faith in
what they can do.

Help people
to become their best.
Have you noticed how
hard it is to dislike people
who like you?

෫෨ ෫෨ ෫෨

Don't deny people the
chance to be themselves.

෫෨ ෫෨ ෫෨

Help people to
continuously improve
themselves; make them
experience it; show
them how to do it;
and have them practice it
till they know how.

Help people
to become their best.

❧ ❧ ❧

The most important
thing is to get people to
believe in themselves.

❧ ❧ ❧

A friend
is a present you
give yourself.

❧ ❧ ❧

When people
work well together,
it's a give and take,
not only take.

The person
who receives the
least number of
positive strokes
is the one who
truly needs them
more than
anyone else.

🐸 🐸 🐸

Nothing binds
us one to the other
like a promise kept.
Nothing divides
us like a
promise broken.
People who
keep their promises,
help others
to keep theirs.

## *The Knit Cap and the World-Class Surfer*

When I think of acts of kindness, I am
reminded of a story told by Rell Sunn, a
world class surfer, also known as the Queen
of Makaha, who was struggling with her
bout with cancer.  She knew one thing about
herself and that was — in spite of her illness
— she wanted to continue to surf. She loved
the ocean and the sport so much and knew it
would be healing for her.  So, one day, soon
after completing her chemotherapy treatment, she headed out to the ocean, her
surfboard in one hand and a knit cap on her
head to cover up her baldness.

She was enjoying the waves when all of a
sudden on her ride into shore, she crashed
beneath the wave.  She came to surface and
the first thing she noticed was that she was
missing her knit cap.  Rell didn't know what
came over her, but a feeling of self-pity
invaded her entire being.  She swam to
shore, leaving her surfboard and cap back in
the ocean.  She ran to her car,  and raced

home. Once home, she just wept uncontrol-
lably. Suddenly, she heard a knock on her
door and there were her friends from the
beach — her surfing companions — with
her surfboard and knit cap. Instantly, she
felt better about herself.

The next day she went back to the sea...
And her surfing. As she sat on her board,
patiently waiting for the right wave ... She
looked to the right and then to the left of her
—and she saw the most incredible sight —
all of the surfers waiting for their waves
were wearing knit caps. Rell was over-
whelmed by the camaraderie and love
shown in that one sincere act. At that
moment, she felt a great impact of their
love, appreciation and support.

How many of us give that kind of support to
people around us in their hour of need? We
all have the opportunity to do that —
Everyday......Everytime.......We come into
contact with a human being.

## *The Goose Story*

Next fall when you see geese heading south
for the winter flying along in a "V" formation, you might be interested in knowing
what science has discovered about why they
fly that way.  It has been learned that as
each bird flaps its wings, it creates an uplift
for the bird immediately following.  By
flying in a "V" formation, the whole flock
adds at least 71% greater flying range than
if each bird flew on its own. (People who
share a common direction and sense of
community can get where they are going
quicker and easier, because they
are traveling on the thrust of one another.)

Whenever a goose falls out of formation, it
suddenly feels the drag and resistance of
trying to go at it alone, and quickly gets
into formation to take advantage of the
lifting power of the bird immediately in
front.  (If we have as much sense as a goose,
we will stay in formation with those who
are headed the same way we are going.)

When the lead goose gets tired, he rotates back in the wing and another goose flies point.
(It pays to take turns doing hard jobs — with people or with geese flying south.)
The geese honk from behind to encourage those up front to keep up their speed. (What do we say when we honk from behind?)

Finally, when a goose gets sick, or is wounded by gun shots and falls out, two geese fall out of formation and follow him down to help and protect him. They stay with him until he is either able to fly or until he is dead, and they then launch out on their own or with another formation to catch up with their group. (If we have the sense of a goose, we will stand by each other like that.)

*– Anonymous*

## *Starfish*

As the old man walked down a Spanish
beach at dawn, he saw ahead of him what
he thought to be a dancer.

The young man was running across the
sand, rhythmically bending down to pick
up a stranded starfish and throw it far
into the sea.

The old man gazed in wonder as the young
soul again and again threw the small starfish
from the sand into the water.

The old man approached him and asked
why he spent so much energy doing what
seemed a waste of time.

The young man explained that the
stranded starfish would die if left until the
morning sun.

"But there are thousands of miles of beach,
and miles and miles of starfish. How can
your effort make any difference?

The young man looked down at the small
starfish in his hand, and as he threw it to
safety in the sea, said,

"It makes a difference to this one!"

– *Anonymous*

Operate with optimism. Develop a positive attitude, a healthy sense of humor and a pattern of effective habits.

When we set a pattern of effective habits in relating to people, we gain their loyalty and love. Many times, the only thing we have is our good word. We can use that to build trust in our relationships and a good reputation to maintain them. When we make a good commitment, we must do everything we can to keep it.

Optimists and pessimists deal with the same challenges in different ways. Optimists are doers, who focus on finding solutions to problems, while pessimists focus emotionally on the problems. The optimist focuses on the heart of the artichoke and not its pricky leaves, the pessimist stares at the pricky leaves, oblivious to the heart of the artichoke. Successful people have courage and are willing to run the risk of failure. They know sooner or later they will reach their goals if they keep trying.

Take whatever you choose to do seriously, but take yourself lightly. Humor is a social lubricant that smooths over frictions that naturally occur when people get together, especially in stress-ful situations. Laugh with people, not at them. Life is just too important to be taken seriously. Humor helps us to rise above the everyday seriousness of our striving and provides a rational and perceptual alternative for facing prob-lems. When we laugh, we tend to be more relaxed, which means we can interact at a more comfortable level.

Research has shown that a good laugh functions the same as vigorous  exercise — increasing the heart rate,

releasing healing hormones and stimulat-
ing muscles.  The body relaxes after
laughing, leaving a person with a sense
of well-being. Laughter has been proven
to have medical benefits and to reduce
stress; and best of all,  it's free and fun
to do.

Quotes to peel by...

Good News!!
Habits are learned,
rather than inherited.
Discard the habits
that aren't working
for you and establish
new ones that support
your goals in life.

≈ ≈ ≈

The two key words that
hold the secret to
motivation: gotta wanna.

≈ ≈ ≈

Reality
has many layers...
enjoy each layer.

Whatever you are
willing to put up
with, is exactly
what you will have.

🐌 🐌 🐌

You are the cause of
everything that
happens to you.
Be careful
what you cause.

🐌 🐌 🐌

You cannot always
control circumstances,
but you can
control your
own thoughts.

It is not the strongest
of the species that
survives, nor the most
intelligent,
but rather the one
most responsive
to change.

🐦 🐦 🐦

We train people how
to treat us.  If we don't
like the treatment, we
need to retrain them.

🐦 🐦 🐦

Treat others the way
you want to be treated,
only do it first.

Know how
you can be a
winner without
making the other
person a loser.

❧ ❧ ❧

The way people see you
behind your back
is how you look
in front of them.

❧ ❧ ❧

Look for positive
things in someone
you dislike.
Get to know
them better.

Everyone likes to
hear the phrase,
" a person of
your standing";
yet no one knows
just what standing
means, but
everyone believes
—or hopes —
he or she has it.

ঌ ঌ ঌ

Celebrate the
differences between us,
but remember the
similarity of
being human.

## *ATTITUDE*

If you think you are beaten, you are.
If you think you dare not, you don't.
If you like to win, but you think you can't,
It is almost certain you won't.

If you think you'll lose, you've lost,
For out in the world we find,
Success begins with a fellow's will —
It's all in the state of mind.

If you think you are outclassed, you are,
You've got to think high to rise,
You've got to be sure of yourself before
You can ever win a prize.

Life's battles don't always go
To the stronger or faster man,
But sooner or later, the person who wins
Is the person *WHO THINKS HE/SHE CAN!*

– *Anonymous*

## *You Become*

Be careful of your thoughts
they become your words.

Be careful of your words
they become your actions.

Be careful of your actions
they become your habits.

Be careful of your habits
they become your character.

Be careful of your character,
it becomes your destiny.

– *Anonymous*

**K**now what to look for and understand what you see. Maximize the moments of truth to create happy memories.

We all have the chance to look at life as a forest full of wonderful living things to experience or as a desert barren of all life. With the exception of a mirage or two happening from time to time in the desert, life there would seem uneventful, frustrating, boring and wasteful. However, how one chooses to go through the process of living will help them to enjoy their experiences or waste their precious moments of life.

It is only when we see through our hearts that we are able to see the beauty of another person, animal or other living thing. Many people miss this extraordinary treat when they view the world, another person or other living things only with their eyes. There is so much more to everything in life. A good example is how we look at a natural piece of wood, with its own design, color, shape, texture, etc.   Some of us might look at that piece of wood and perhaps acknowledge its beauty and unusual characteristics.

However, a person whose heart is touched through the vision of what that wood could become, begins to see it as a piece of art or something that can be shaped into a practical and useful thing to enjoy.   Then, goes about bringing that vision to reality.

When you seriously look at life, you begin to realize that it is a succession of moments —the collection of which is your entire life.  How we live each moment will determine the quality of our life.  Through our experiences living those moments, we make memories. Memories are continuously and constantly being produced and recorded by our minds. When we live wonderful moments, those times are somehow etched in our brains forever — as positive, nurturing and reinforcing forces reminding us that we are loved and cared about by other people.

Negative thoughts are also recorded for eternity and have a damaging impact on our lives. With a reserve of happy memories, we can retrieve and relive those moments to help sustain and nourish us through difficult and empty times.

As memory makers we must look beyond what we see and bring value to those people and things that help to make our lives easier and happy. After

all, what we have is worth whatever
worth we place in it.

Quotes to "peel" by...

We see things not as they
are — but as we are.

❧ ❧ ❧

To understand the heart
and mind of a person,
look not at what
the person has already
achieved, but at
what he aspires to do.

❧ ❧ ❧

Tune in to people.
Give them
what they need
so they can feel
good about
themselves.

Make people feel
welcomed, needed
and appreciated.
The greatest hunger that
people have is to be needed,
wanted and loved.

ॐ ॐ ॐ

Be involved in the
conspiracy of caring.
When you care,
other people will
care too.
It is most interesting
to note that no matter how
smart or accomplished
you are, people don't care
how much you know,
until they know
you care

They say
if a person
understands oneself,
that person understands
all people.
However,
when a person
loves people,
that person learns
something about oneself.
If you want
to find out more
about yourself,
observe
your neighbor,
but if you want to
understand more
about people,
look onto
yourself.

When someone
close to us dies,
we cry for ourselves
and the joy that has
been taken from us.
It is then
that we remember
the person's special gift
that we will never
have again.

🐦 🐦 🐦

When your tendency
is to blame another
person for how you feel,
look in the mirror and
remind yourself that
who you see is the only
person responsible
for your happiness.

We become
what we think.
Think positive.
Think big.
Think healthy.
Think the best of you.

≈ ≈ ≈

We preserve mangos,
cucumbers, other fruits
and vegetables so we
can have them
when they are
out of season.
Why don't we
preserve our
happy memories
so we can have
them when we
need them?

Balance
your priorities of
give-and-take
more wisely.

❧ ❧ ❧

Be a good
forgetter.
Life
dictates it
and success
in your
relationships
demands it.

❧ ❧ ❧

## *A Mother's Rainbow*

Many of us look at a rainbow and are in
awe with it's beauty.  No matter how many
times we see a rainbow we can still see its
majestically-colored body bending in an
arch inviting our minds to wander at
another psychological level, even taking us
mentally to a more beautiful and peaceful
place — perhaps, a place most of us iden-
tify with as heaven.

It is said that the pot of gold is at one end of
the rainbow, yet no one has actually veri-
fied that statement.  Perhaps it is better to
think of it as symbolic of the significance of
the rainbow itself — so that people will
look at both sides of the rainbow trying to
figure out which side the pot of gold is on.
In reality they are looking at the colors,
form and design, or the beauty of the
rainbow in its entirety.

It's magnificence is unmatched by any man-made palette on which colors are deliberately placed.

It is no wonder that a mother looking at a rainbow, would think about the powerful and lasting positive effect it could have on her child.

The story about such a mother was told to us at a seminar. The young seminar leader was speaking about his own mother. He said that he and his mother had a very close relationship ever since he was a toddler. His father was a traveling salesperson, so a lot of his time was spent with his mother.

His mother took great interest in his up-bringing and everyday activities. She supported him in whatever he was doing. She never missed any of his football games or practice sessions. His mother was his best friend, his confidante — he told her everything and she shared a lot with him as well.

After dinner one night, his mother told him that she needed to discuss something very important. His mother said she had gone to the doctor that day and found out that she had a life-threatening disease and had only three months to live. She told him that she wanted those three months to be the very best days of their lives. She wanted him to ask her all the questions he had for her, and for her to hear all about his hopes and dreams.

Their days and months were filled with joy, yet shrouded with sadness. He recalled that one of his most vivid memories was his mother telling him that she wanted him to remember how much she loved him everytime he saw a rainbow.

The three months passed with swiftness.

One day at football practice he noticed that she wasn't there. A terrible feeling came over him and he raced home only to find an ambulance taking his mother away.
She had died before he could say his final good-bye.

He said that rainbows are very meaningful to him. No matter where he travels through-out the world, when he sees a rainbow, he has a special feeling. However, he said that Hawaii was his favorite place to visit because— as he put it, " There are so many beautiful rainbows to remind me how much I am loved."

*Excel within yourself by always being your best self. Your uniqueness is your greatest asset.*

You are somebody special. There is no one exactly like you in this world. Find your gift in life — as early in life as you can — and touch people with your uniqueness. Don't sabotage yourself by trying to be someone else. Be proud of who you are. You are the best at being yourself, nobody can do it better than you can. In all that you do, expect the best and you'll get the best. The positive power within you is unlimited. If any barrier to success exists, it is only in your own mind — your attitude toward yourself and your self-confidence.

Be whatever you want, but always be you. Don't try to be someone else, because the minute you try, you decrease your chance of being the unique person that you are. Don't be a carbon copy....you were born an original, keep your value!  The nice thing is that you can't fail at being yourself.

We can't give others what we don't have.  Therefore, we must find, develop, and use our inner power to attain our fullest potential and share that with others. Can you imagine if Picasso, Maria Callas, Mikhail Borishnikof, Elvis Presley, Oprah Winfrey, Al Pacino or Michael Jordan — just to name a few extordinary people — had not found their special talents? Certainly, we would have missed out on some very wonderful experiences their uniqueness brought to our lives.

The human mind is powerful in helping us to cope and excel in all situations.  Program yourself to think the best, do the best , share your best, and celebrate your successes. The first step towards personal excellence is to focus on being the best you can be. After that, make sure you give your best everytime with everyone.

Quotes to "peel" by...

Excellence
is an inside job.
Manage yourself
well so you can help
others effectively.

᠊᠊᠊ ᠊᠊᠊ ᠊᠊᠊

Be what you are
and become
what you are
capable of
becoming.
A caterpillar
can only become a
butterfly,
not a cow.
A flower
on a mango tree
turns into a mango,
and not a grapefruit.

If you become like
someone else,
you'll always be
number 2.

᠄᠄ ᠄᠄ ᠄᠄

Be kind to yourself.
The emotion
you bring
to a situation
is what
people will feel.

᠄᠄ ᠄᠄ ᠄᠄

Experience
is a good teacher.
Learn well
the lessons of
life.

Self-knowledge is the
basis of all knowledge.
Get to know
yourself better.

❧ ❧ ❧

Gaining the respect
and confidence of others
depends upon how you
feel about yourself.

❧ ❧ ❧

You are only effective
if you are yourself.
If you aren't
comfortable
with that,
then you're in
the wrong place.

To love oneself is the
beginning of a
lifelong romance.

🐸 🐸 🐸

Power is like kindness.
If you give some of
yours away, your supply
does not diminish.
You only become
more powerful.

🐸 🐸 🐸

There is only one
corner of the universe
you can be certain
of improving;
and that's your
own self.

The key to personal
excellence is not
knowledge,
but how you apply
what you know.
It's not what you
know that makes you
successful in your life,
but what you do with
what you know.
The real test is when
you actually do it.

❧ ❧ ❧

It's not how
smart you are,
but how you are smart.

❧ ❧ ❧

## *Expect the Best*

What's exciting about life is that
every morning offers a brand-new
day with unlimited possibilities.
Yesterday's mistakes and regrets
belong to yesterday.  Today is a
clean slate, a chance to start over,
to do or become anything you
want, a chance to go for it!
So jump into life with both feet!
Go forward, head held high,
expecting the best...you may be
surprised at how often that's
exactly what you'll get.

*Anonymous*

## *Change*

When I was young and free and my imagination had no limits, I dreamed of changing the world. As I grew older and wiser, I discovered the world would not change, so I shortened my sights somewhat and decided to change only my country.

But it, too, seemed immovable.

As I grew into my twilight years, in one last desperate attempt, I settled for changing only my family, those closest to me, but alas, they would have none of it.

And now as I lie on my deathbed, I suddenly realize: If I had only changed myself first, then by example I would have changed my family.

From their inspiration and encouragement, I would then have been able to better my country and, who knows, I may have even changed the world.

– *Anonymous*

### *My Prayer*

Dear God,
Help me to be a sport
in this little game of life.
I don't ask for any place
in the lineup;
Play me where you need me.
I only ask for the stuff to give you a
hundred percent of what I've got.
If all the hard drives come my way,
I thank you for the compliment.
Help me remember that you won't
let anything come my way that
you and I together can't handle.
And help me take the bad
breaks as part of the game.
Help me to be thankful for them.
And God, help me always play
on the square,
No matter what the other players do.
Help me come clean.
Help me see that often the best of

the game is helping other guys.
Help me be a "regular fellow"
with the other players.
Finally God, if fate seems to
uppercut me with both hands,
And I'm laid up on the shelf,
Help me take that part of the
game also.
Help me not to whisper or squeal
that the game was a frame-up
Or that I had a raw deal.
When, in the dusk, I get
the final bell, I ask for no lying
complimentary stones.
I'd only like to know that you
feel I've been a good guy!

*– Brother Robert Bader*

# Seminars & Keynotes

More than 25,000 individuals from Las Vegas to Australia have already benefited from Dr. Wheeler's exciting and informative seminars.

We invite and encourage you to contact us to learn more about our winning programs designed to teach participants the attitudes, knowledge and skills necessary to "take charge" of their lives.

Our philosophical basis is to help people feel good about themselves and others, so they can produce positive results.

*If you would like more information about our programs, please write or call for a complete description:*

TheHumanConnection

1210 Auahi Street, Suite 231
Honolulu, Hawaii 96814
Phone (808)597-8166
Fax (808)593-8867
Toll-free (800)471-9808

# Ordering Information

***"Ain't Life an Artichoke?..."***
It's easy to order additional copies of this
dynamic book. They make great gifts, too!
$7.95+$3.00 s/h


*"Bringing the Aloha Spirit into the
Workplace"* What is the Aloha Spirit?
What is its impact on interpersonal
relationships in the workplace?
The answers to these and other questions
are found in this audioworkshop by
Dr. Linda Andrade Wheeler. (30 min.)
$12.95+$3.00 s/h


**FREE Successories® Full-Color Catalog**
*Call us today for your free copy!*

SUCCESSORIES®

1200 Ala Moana Blvd.
Honolulu, Hawaii 96814
Phone (808) 593-8812
Fax (808)593-8867
Toll-free (800)471-9808